CULTURAL CONTRIBUTIONS FROM

THE MIDDLE EAST

HOSPITALS, ALGEBRA, AND MORE

GREAT CULTURES,
GREAT IDEAS

MADELINE TYLER

PowerKiDS
press

Published in 2019 by The Rosen Publishing Group, Inc.
29 East 21st Street, New York, NY 10010

Cataloging-in-Publication Data

Names: Tyler, Madeline.
Title: Cultural contributions from the Middle East: hospitals, algebra, and more / Madeline Tyler.
Description: New York : PowerKids Press, 2019. I Series: Great cultures, great ideas I Includes glossary and index.
Identifiers: LCCN ISBN 9781538338346 (pbk.) I ISBN 9781538338339 (library bound) I ISBN 9781538338353 (6 pack)
Subjects: LCSH: Middle East--Juvenile literature. I Middle East--Social life and customs--Juvenile literature. I Civilization,
Western--Middle Eastern influences
Classification: LCC DS44.T954 2019 I DDC 956--dc23

Written by: Madeline Tyler
Edited by: Holly Duhig
Designed by: Gareth Liddington

Photo credits
Abbreviations: l-left, r-right, b-bottom, t-top, c-center, m-middle.

Front Cover – DutchScenery, Syda Productions, alge calc, elbud, AnastasiaSonne, Sergey Mironov, Azat1976, Ilia Torlin, 2 – AstroStar.
4 – stocker1970, Jakkarin Apikornrat, Creative-Touch, AJP, Sirisak Chantorn, Memory Stockphoto, piyaphong, 5 – AJ Frames, DisobeyAr,
Sata Production, Jennifer Lam, Kamil Macniak, 6 – Magdanatka, I am Corona, hxduyl, 7 – sebasnoo, Heath Doman, Maximumvector,
charnsitr, 9 – adike, PSboom, 9 – Fedor Selivanov, 10 – NormanEinstein, Nebojsa Markovic, 11 – TambulaRogeriana, OGdesign, Icons vector,
Andrey_Kuzmin, Hermann Vollrat Hilprecht, 12 – ColinCramm, Michaela Stejskalova, 13 – Aleksandr Semenov, Josell7, sundatoon, 14 –
Victor Jiang, Andrey Prokhorov, 15 – Juan Aunion, Brian Maudsley, Seyyed Hossein Nasr, 16 – kuzina, Africa Studio, 17 – titov dmitriy,
Images4ever, 18 – saiko3p, Suzyderkins, 19 – Africa Studio, selinofoto, 20 – Yusnizam Yusof, WikimediaCommons, 21 – szefet, Eng,
Bilal Izaddin, 22 – Jan van der Hoeven, kaesezo, Geni, 23 – Helder Almeida, elbud, 24 – Sanit Fuangnakhon, Michal Knitl, 25 –
ChiccoDodiFC, Sotheby, USAID, 26 – HandmadePictures, stockcreations, 27 – Slawomir Fajer, Vigen M, Gossip, 28 – Mohammed Tareq,
29 – Konstantin Stepanenko, 30 – Denis Burdin, Michael Portter11

Images are courtesy of Shutterstock.com. With thanks to Getty Images, Thinkstock Photo and iStockphoto.

Manufactured in the United States of America

CPSIA Compliance Information: Batch #CSPK18: For Further Information contact
Rosen Publishing, New York, New York at 1-800-237-9932.

CONTENTS

Words that look like **this** are explained in the glossary on page 31.

WHAT IS CULTURE?

If you were to travel around the world, visiting lots of countries on the way, you would probably notice that certain things around you would not be the same as they are at home. The countries and places you visit, and the people you meet, would have different languages, customs, and ways of doing things. The food might be different, the way people dress might be different, and even the laws and rules might be different to what you know at home. All of these things, when put together, make up what we call the culture of a place.

A HOUSE IN CHINA MIGHT LOOK VERY DIFFERENT THAN ONE IN THE UK!

WHAT MAKES UP A CULTURE?

Shared ideas and traditions that make up a culture can include:

LAWS	HOLIDAYS
FOOD	FAMILIES
LEADERS	SCHOOLS
SYMBOLS	SPECIAL BUILDINGS
BELIEFS	HOSPITALS
CEREMONIES	ENTERTAINMENT

A culture can also be shared by a group of people who might not live near each other, but have shared values and a way of life. For example, people who all like the same thing, like certain music or hobbies, can be said to share a culture. People who all belong to the same religion can be said to share a culture, no matter where they live.

BEAUTIFUL HENNA TATTOOS ARE PART OF INDIAN CULTURE. MANY INDIAN BRIDES AROUND THE WORLD PRACTICE THIS CULTURAL TRADITION.

Our culture is a big part of our identity. Having a distinctive culture is what makes places or people unique. Knowing you belong to a particular culture is a good feeling. It's nice to share our culture with other people. If we are in a culture we recognize, we understand what to do or how to act.

DIFFERENT CULTURES GREET EACH OTHER IN DIFFERENT WAYS – A HANDSHAKE, A BOW, OR EVEN A KISS!

GLOBAL CULTURE

Even though every culture is different and has many things that make it unique, many cultures also have lots of things in common. We can learn a lot from other cultures, and share the things we know and like. In the past, when people started traveling and visiting other cultures, they began to swap and share their food, traditions, and knowledge, and people started to adopt things from other cultures into their own. For example, British people see drinking tea as part of their cultural identity—but tea is originally from China and is also an important part of Japanese culture.

AFTERNOON TEA, WITH CAKES AND SANDWICHES, IS A TRADITIONAL PART OF ENGLISH CULTURE.

IN JAPAN, THE TEA CEREMONY IS AN IMPORTANT CULTURAL RITUAL.

TEA WAS ORIGINALLY FROM CHINA AND ORIGINATED DURING THE SHANG DYNASTY.

It is also really interesting to explore other cultures and discover new and exciting ways of doing things! We can share our ideas and learn new things when cultures meet.

MY CULTURE, YOUR CULTURE, OUR CULTURE

Adopting ideas from other cultures can lead to really interesting results. Many cultures take inspiration from others and adapt and change their traditions and customs to make them their own. Putting two ideas from two different cultures together can produce new and exciting things. Did you know that a pizza in Italy will look very different from a pizza in the US? Italians introduced pizza, a traditional Italian dish, to the Americans living in the US. A traditional Italian pizza has a thin, crispy crust, and lots of tomato, but only a small amount of mozzarella cheese. An American pizza has a thick, fluffy base, is smothered in cheese, and can have lots of different toppings – meats, fish, even pineapple! Both cultures share a love for pizza, but each culture has their own way of doing things!

WHICH PIZZA DO YOU PREFER? ITALIAN, AMERICAN, OR MAYBE A SLICE OF EACH?

TRADITIONAL ITALIAN PIZZA

AMERICAN PIZZA

WHERE IS THE MIDDLE EAST?

The Middle East is a very large area. It is made up of countries from Africa, Asia, and Europe, and can be found in the Northern and Eastern **hemispheres**. There are many countries in the Middle East, and they all have different cultures.

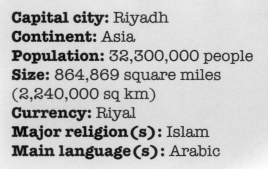

Morocco

Capital city: Rabat
Continent: Africa
Population: 35,900,000 people
Size: 172,414 square miles
(446,550 sq km)
Currency: Dirham
Major religion(s): Islam
Main language(s): Arabic, **Berber**, French, Spanish

Saudi Arabia

Capital city: Riyadh
Continent: Asia
Population: 32,300,000 people
Size: 864,869 square miles
(2,240,000 sq km)
Currency: Riyal
Major religion(s): Islam
Main language(s): Arabic

Iraq

Capital city: Baghdad
Continent: Asia
Population: 37,000,000 people
Size: 169,235 square miles
(438,317 sq km)
Currency: Iraqi dinar
Major religion(s): Islam
Main language(s): Arabic, Kurdish

CAN YOU SPOT WHERE THE MIDDLE EAST IS?

Iran

Capital city: Tehran
Continent: Asia
Population: 75,000,000 people
Size: 637,069 square miles
(1,650,000 sq km)
Currency: Rial
Major religion(s): Islam
Main language(s): Persian

RIYADH, SAUDI ARABIA

The Ancient Middle East is sometimes called the Ancient Near East. It includes the **civilizations** of Mesopotamia, Persia, Anatolia, the Levant, and ancient Egypt.

Lots of inventions and discoveries came out of this area because of the many rivers running through it. The area between these rivers is sometimes referred to as the Fertile Crescent. Water is extremely important for drinking, growing food, washing, and cleaning. This made it the perfect area for **settlements** and growing crops.

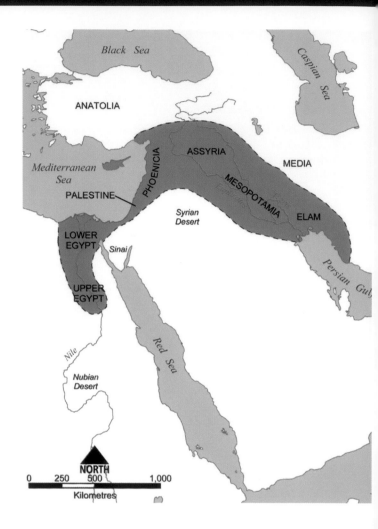

RIVER NILE

Ancient	Modern
Mesopotamia	Iraq and Syria
Persia	Iran
Anatolia	Turkey
The Levant	Syria, Lebanon, Israel, Palestine, Jordan
Ancient Egypt	Egypt
Arabia	Bahrain, Kuwait, Oman, Qatar, Saudi Arabia, United Arab Emirates, Yemen, Iraq, Jordan

MAPS

Have you ever used a map of a town or city? If you have, you may have noticed how different parts of land are drawn differently. Landmarks also have different symbols to represent them. Here are some examples:

TWO LINES DRAWN CLOSE TOGETHER SHOW A RIVER OR CANAL.

SQUARES OR RECTANGLES SYMBOLIZE A TEMPLE.

FLOWING RIVER

BUILDING

PICNIC AREA

Babylon was a town in ancient Mesopotamia. People in ancient Babylon were very advanced **cartographers**. They used accurate techniques for surveying the land and symbols to represent different places on their maps.

MUHAMMAD AL-IDRISI CREATED THE TABULA ROGERIANA MAP IN 1154. IT WAS THE MOST ACCURATE WORLD MAP FOR 300 YEARS!

TELLING THE TIME

There are 60 seconds in a minute, 60 minutes in an hour, and 12 hours on an analog clock. But why is 60 such an important number? Because it has 12 **factors**: 1, 2, 3, 4, 5, 6, 10, 12, 15, 20, 30, and 60. This means that 60 is a multiple of each of these numbers. This is important because it means one hour can be divided evenly into sections of 30 minutes, 20 minutes, 15 minutes, 12 minutes, 10 minutes, 6 minutes, 5 minutes, 4 minutes, 3 minutes, 2 minutes and 1 minute.

TRY IT ON THIS CLOCK!

A number system that uses 60 as a base number like this is called **sexagesimal** number system. It was created by people in the ancient Middle East and is still used for measuring time, angles, and geographic **coordinates**.

WE USUALLY SPLIT AN HOUR INTO SECTIONS OF 5 MINUTES, 15 MINUTES, AND 30 MINUTES.

CAN YOU BE A DETECTIVE DECODER?

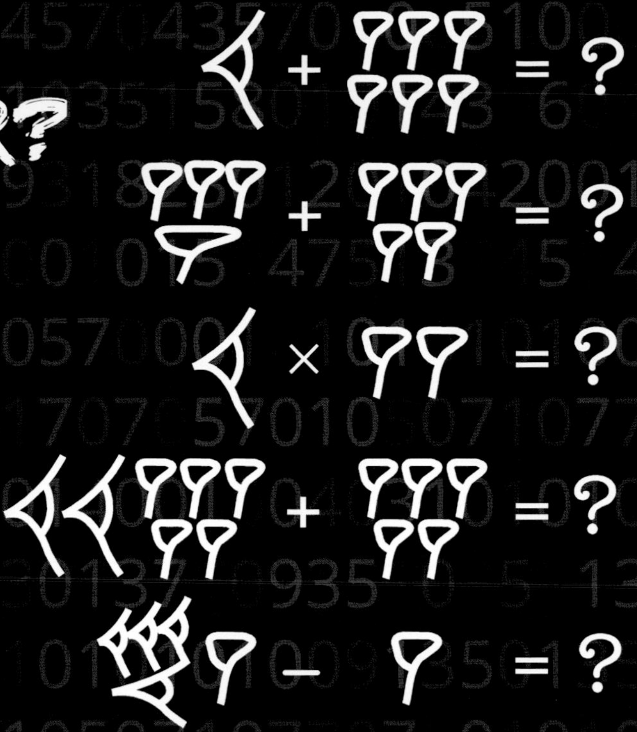

These symbols are actually numbers and were developed by the Babylonians! Use the key to crack the code and open the safe!

$$\text{𒌋} + \frac{\text{𒐖𒐖𒐖}}{\text{𒐖𒐖𒐖}} = ?$$

$$\frac{\text{𒐖𒐖𒐖}}{\text{𒐖𒐖}} + \frac{\text{𒐖𒐖𒐖}}{\text{𒐖𒐖}} = ?$$

$$\text{𒌋} \times \text{𒐖𒐖} = ?$$

$$\text{𒌋𒌋}\frac{\text{𒐖𒐖𒐖}}{\text{𒐖𒐖}} + \frac{\text{𒐖𒐖𒐖}}{\text{𒐖𒐖}} = ?$$

$$\text{𒐏𒐖} - \text{𒐖} = ?$$

BABYLONIAN NUMBERS ARE WRITTEN IN CUNEIFORM. THIS MEANS THAT THEY ARE WEDGE-SHAPED.

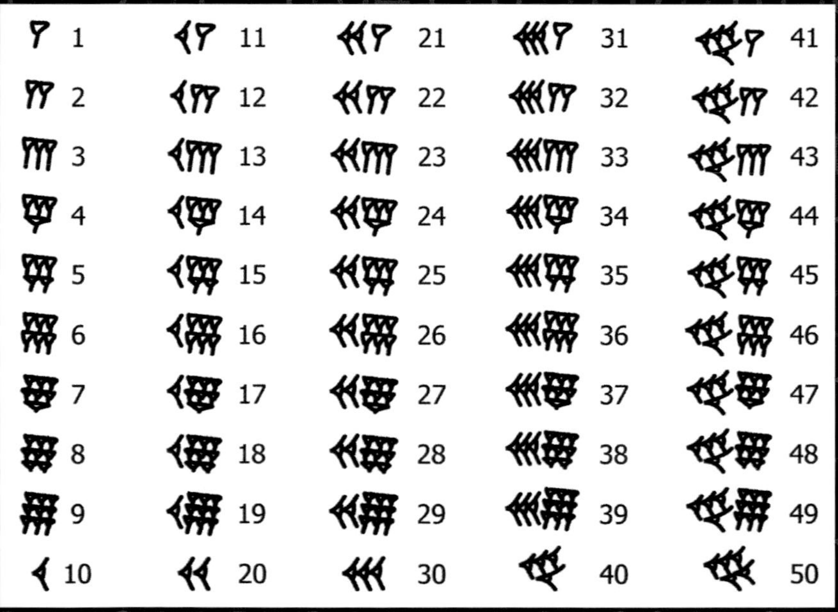

ANSWERS ARE PRINTED UPSIDE DOWN AT THE BOTTOM OF PAGE 32!

𒁹 1	𒌋𒁹 11	𒌋𒌋𒁹 21	𒌍𒁹 31	𒐏𒁹 41
𒈫 2	𒌋𒈫 12	𒌋𒌋𒈫 22	𒌍𒈫 32	𒐏𒈫 42
𒐏 3	𒌋𒐏 13	𒌋𒌋𒐏 23	𒌍𒐏 33	𒐏𒐏 43
𒃻 4	𒌋𒃻 14	𒌋𒌋𒃻 24	𒌍𒃻 34	𒐏𒃻 44
� 5	𒌋 15	𒌋𒌋 25	𒌍 35	𒐏 45
𒍢 6	𒌋 16	𒌋𒌋 26	𒌍 36	𒐏 46
�seven 7	𒌋 17	𒌋𒌋 27	𒌍 37	𒐏 47
𒂊 8	𒌋 18	𒌋𒌋 28	𒌍 38	𒐏 48
𒐲 9	𒌋 19	𒌋𒌋 29	𒌍 39	𒐏 49
𒌋 10	𒌋𒌋 20	𒌍 30	𒐏 40	𒐏 50

BIG NUMBERS, LITTLE NUMBERS

THE BABYLONIANS WERE THE FIRST PEOPLE TO USE THE POSITION OF THEIR NUMBERS TO SHOW WHICH ONES ARE BIGGER IN VALUE. THIS IS CALLED A POSITIONAL NUMERAL SYSTEM. IT'S HOW WE KNOW THAT 21 IS BIGGER THAN 12!

13

ASTRONOMY AND CALENDARS

ASTRONOMY

Astronomy is the study of things in our universe, such as planets and stars, and is important for the followers of Islam. By studying the Sun and stars, early Muslims were able to work out the exact times for prayer, the beginning of **Ramadan** and the direction of the city **Mecca**, which is the direction Muslims face when praying. Prayer is a very important part of Islam. Muslims learn that Allah commanded them to pray at five very specific times every day.

During the 8th century AD, Baghdad, the capital city of Iraq, was a world center of culture and learning. It was home to libraries and government buildings, and the study of subjects like **philosophy**, science, and medicine was encouraged. During this time, people also used the minarets of mosques as a way to study the planets and stars.

MINARETS ARE VERY HIGH TOWERS THAT ARE CONNECTED TO MOSQUES.

CALENDARS

Accurately telling the time is important in Islam, especially for working out prayer times. The ritual prayer of Muslims is called Salat and is the second **Pillar of Islam**. Observing the sunrise and sunset was an ancient method of working out the time. An important invention that helped with this was the astrolabe, a device that was used for measuring angles.

The astrolabe allowed people to work out the times of sunrise and sunset, the rising times of certain stars, and how to calculate **latitude**.

MEDIEVAL ARABIC ASTROLABE

CLOSE-UP OF AN ASTROLABE

AL-BIRUNI WAS AN IRANIAN ASTRONOMER. THIS IS HIS DIAGRAM EXPLAINING THE PHASES OF THE MOON.

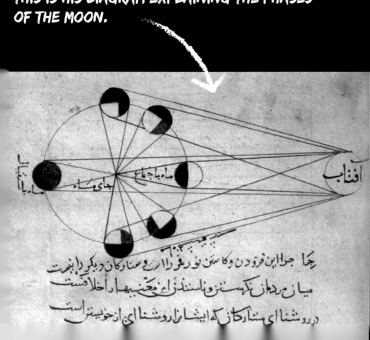

The Babylonians used astronomy to create a very early **lunar calendar**. They observed the **orbit** of the moon and its phases to produce a 12-month calendar, similar to the Gregorian calendar that is used today.

THE BABYLONIANS HAD TO SOMETIMES ADD AN EXTRA MONTH TO THEIR CALENDAR. THIS WAS TO KEEP IT IN LINE WITH THE SEASONS.

SOAP

Whether you are a bubbly bather or a speedy scrubber, everyone uses soap to get clean. The first people to use soap were the people of Mesopotamia almost 5,000 years ago! This early soap was made from mixing animal fats with wood ash and water! Although it might not sound clean, people used this soap to wash fabrics like wool and cotton.

THE BABYLONIANS KEPT THEIR SOAP IN CLAY CONTAINERS.

Many hundreds of years later, around the 6th century BC, the Babylonians started making soap with **cypress extracts** and sesame oil. This meant that the soap did more than just clean – it smelled nice too! Most modern soap is **scented**, but the soap we use now usually smells of fruits or flowers instead of cypress or sesame.

SOAP BOTTLES COME IN LOTS OF DIFFERENT SHAPES AND SIZES.

PERFUME

Perfume has been around for thousands of years, but people have not always worn it like they do now. It was originally used in religious ceremonies, with the burning of incense and **aromatic** herbs, like frankincense and myrrh.

PERFUME MAKING WAS A SUCCESS IN THE MIDDLE EAST BECAUSE THE PEOPLE WHO LIVED THERE HAD ACCESS TO A WIDE VARIETY OF SPICES, HERBS, AND FLOWERS.

ARABIAN INCENSE BURNER

Perfume making would not have been possible without Tapputi. Tapputi was a woman in Mesopotamia who developed methods for **extracting** scents from raw materials to be used in perfumes.

Two Arabian **chemists**, Jābir ibn Ḥayyān and Al-Kindi, carried out more work on perfume making in what is now known as Iraq. They learned more about extracting scents and how to mix these different smells together. Perfume was transported from Arabia to Europe in the 11th century, and now it can be found all over the world!

HOSPITALS

The Greek and Roman empires were the first places where a special building was dedicated to healing people. These places were like temples and were often associated with a specific god. Hospitals first appeared in Baghdad in AD 932, and were often called bimaristans, meaning "place for ill people."

THESE ARE THE RUINS OF THE SANCTUARY OF ASCLEPIUS IN EPIDAURUS, GREECE.

The new hospitals in the Islamic Empire were revolutionary because they wanted to treat everyone, no matter what their background or religion was. The hospitals were free and open to everyone. They provided medical and **surgical** treatments, care for the elderly, and treatment for **mental illness**.

ASCLEPIUS IS THE GOD OF MEDICINE AND HEALING IN ANCIENT GREEK MYTHOLOGY. THE WORLD HEALTH ORGANIZATION AND AMERICAN MEDICAL RESPONSE STILL USE THE ROD OF ASCLEPIUS IN THEIR LOGOS.

Unlike Christian hospitals, which remained very religious until the 1800s, hospitals in the Islamic Empire were **secular**. Muslim, Jewish, and Christian doctors could all work in the same hospital, and both men and women cared for the patients. After 100 years, hospitals in the Middle East were very large, so they set up doctors' surgeries and pharmacies.

If you want to become a doctor, you must first go to college and learn from other doctors in a university hospital. Medical education was very important in Islamic hospitals, and the first hospital where you could learn to become a doctor was in Baghdad. Medical students read texts about medicine, received practical training, and even observed patients. Students learned about **symptoms** and treatments, and were taught to look for the color and temperature of a patient's skin.

LIBRARIES

The first Muslim libraries were built to look after the Koran, which is the Holy Book of Islam, and the Traditions of the Muhammad. These Islamic writings were stored in mosques. Later on, mosques began storing less religious books on philosophy, mathematics, and science. In the 9th century AD, a paper mill was set up in Baghdad. After learning how to make paper from the Chinese, more books could be made and the libraries could grow. Public libraries, or "Halls of Science," began appearing, with the aim of spreading knowledge.

THIS IS A SKETCH OF THE HOUSE OF WISDOM.

THE HOUSE OF WISDOM

An important library in the Middle East at this time was the House of Wisdom in Baghdad. It was founded by Caliph Harun al-Rashid around the end of the 8th century. After around 50 years, the House of Wisdom had the largest collection of books in the world.

COLLEGES

The House of Wisdom was a library and a place for research and education. Inventions and knowledge from different cultures came together in the House of Wisdom. Paper-making technology was learned from China, and European texts were translated into Arabic for Arabic speakers.

THE MATHEMATICIAN AL-KHWĀRIZMĪ WORKED IN THE HOUSE OF WISDOM. HE IS OFTEN CONSIDERED THE FATHER OF ALGEBRA.

MEN AND WOMEN OF DIFFERENT FAITHS AND ETHNICITIES WERE ALL WELCOME AT THE HOUSE OF WISDOM.

Translators, scientists, and writers traveled to the House of Wisdom to discuss ideas and theories with each other, much like colleges today. It attracted great thinkers from across Asia and the Middle East. The scholars could study mathematics, astronomy, medicine, chemistry, and geography there.

OP-WHAT?

Optics sounds complicated, but it is something we rely on every day. It is the study of light and it helps to explain how we see things.

People have been thinking about how light works for thousands of years, observing how light is bent, or **refracted**, in water.

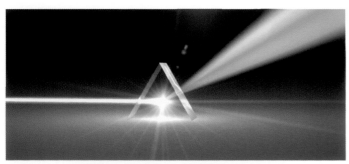

GLASS PYRAMIDS REFRACT LIGHT AND PRODUCE RAINBOWS.

TRY IT! PUT A PENCIL IN A GLASS OF WATER AND SEE WHAT HAPPENS. IT WILL LOOK BENT BECAUSE THE GLASS REFRACTS THE LIGHT.

Ibn Al-Haytham is often called the Father of Modern Optics because of his book, the *Book of Optics*. Ibn Al-Haytham studied shadows, **eclipses** and rainbows, and came up with the laws of refraction.

One early example of optics in the Middle East is the Nimrud lens. This lens is thought to be the oldest in the world and was created from a polished crystal in Assyria around 2,700 years ago. It could have been used as a magnifying glass or for starting fires, but no one is completely sure.

THIS IS THE NIMRUD LENS.

MAKE YOUR OWN PINHOLE CAMERA!

TURN THE BOOK UPSIDE DOWN AND USE A MIRROR TO READ THESE TOP-SECRET INSTRUCTIONS!

THIS IS WHAT A PINHOLE CAMERA LOOKS LIKE.

YOU WILL NEED

- A round container
- Pencil or push pin
- Wax paper
- Scissors
- Tape
- Blanket

METHOD

1. Get your clean, round container. Make a little hole in the bottom of the container with your pencil or push pin. Ask a grown-up for help if this is a bit tricky.

2. Cut some paper to fit over the top of your container. Fix it in place with some tape.

3. Cover yourself and your pinhole camera with a blanket. Slide the lens end of the camera out of the blanket, but make sure the rest is still covered!

4. Look through the wax paper at your friends. What do they look like through the camera?

PERSIAN CARPETS

Do you have a rug in your house? Some rugs are fluffy while others are more colorful. Rugs come in lots of different shapes, sizess and colors, and can be used all around someone's home.

IN 2007, CARPET WEAVERS IN IRAN MADE THE LARGEST CARPET IN THE WORLD! IT WAS THE SIZE OF A SOCCER FIELD AND TOOK A YEAR AND A HALF TO MAKE!

ROLLS OF PERSIAN CARPETS IN IRAN.

Persian carpets are very important to Iranian art and culture. People have been weaving carpets in Iran for thousands of years, and each rug can take anything from several months to over a year to complete.

Persian carpets are traditionally hand-knotted and are made from cotton and wool. Persian carpets are unique because many of them are handmade, so no two carpets look the same! Each design is very special and is seen as a work of art.

AFGHAN RUGS

Afghanistan is also well known for creating beautiful handmade carpets. Just like in Iran, carpet weaving is a big part of Afghan culture. Afghanistan is surrounded by countries with many different cultures which have inspired Afghan carpet weavers' use of colors and patterns.

Like Persian carpets, Afghan rugs are often made of cotton and wool. The weavers use natural dyes from vegetables to color the fabrics. The rugs often show images from traditional Afghan life. Persian and Afghan carpets are very popular around the world. Do any of these carpets look familiar?

A COMMON DESIGN IN AFGHAN RUGS IS THE BUKHARA PRINT ON A RED BACKGROUND.

THIS IS A TRADITIONAL ADRASKAN AFGHAN RUG.

FOOD

Lots of popular foods were first made in the Middle East. You may not realize it, but you have probably tried some before! Lebanese, Israeli, and Turkish cuisines are particularly popular in many countries outside of the Middle East.

HUMMUS

Have you ever tried hummus? It is a tasty dip made from chickpeas and other ingredients. It has been around for hundreds of years and no one is sure which country in the Middle East made it first. Hummus has changed a lot over the years and is now a popular dish in many countries, with some people even making chocolate hummus!

HUMMUS AND FALAFEL ARE POPULAR DISHES IN THE MIDDLE EAST.

FALAFEL

Another popular food made from chickpeas is falafel. Although the Egyptians may have come up with the recipe for falafel, it was made popular in Israel. Falafel is usually eaten inside a pita or a flatbread, topped with leafy greens and vegetables.

PITA BREAD

Pita bread dates back around 4,000 years to ancient Mesopotamia. Pita is an important food in the Middle East. It can be used to scoop hummus or wrap falafel. You can also open a pita and fill it with delicious foods like shawarma. Have you ever tried pita bread?

THIS PITA IS FILLED WITH FALAFEL.

IN TURKEY, THEY CALL TURKISH DELIGHT LOKUM. THIS MEANS "MOUTHFUL."

TURKISH DELIGHT

Turkish delight was created over 300 years ago and is now a popular sweet across the Middle East, Europe, and the US. Turkish delight can come in a variety of flavors including rosewater, orange, and lemon. Turkish delight can be made with nuts, and sometimes it is even covered with chocolate! Some people believe that modern jelly beans were inspired by Turkish delight.

SHAWARMA IS MEAT GRILLED ON A SPIT FOR UP TO A DAY!

BURJ KHALIFA

Dubai is the largest city in the United Arab Emirates with a population of almost 3,000,000 people. Many of its buildings are very **iconic**. One of these is the Burj Khalifa, a skyscraper that is currently the tallest building in the world! It is 2,716 feet (828 m) tall. That is the same as two Empire State Buildings!

DUBAI HOLDS THE GUINNESS WORLD RECORD FOR THE HIGHEST FIREWORKS ON A BUILDING. FIREWORKS WERE RELEASED FROM THE BURJ KHALIFA ON NEW YEAR'S EVE 2015.

BURJ KHALIFA, DUBAI

Here are some records that the Burj Khalifa has broken:
- Tallest free-standing structure in the world.
- Highest number of stories in the world.
- Highest occupied floor in the world.
- Highest outdoor observation deck in the world.
- Elevator with the longest travel distance in the world.
- Tallest service elevator in the world.

PALM JUMEIRAH

Another interesting construction in Dubai is the Palm Jumeirah. The Palm is a collection of manmade islands that are designed to look like a palm tree. These islands were made from sand, stones, and boulders, and took eight years to finish.

PALM JUMEIRAH WAS PART OF A RECORD-BREAKING FIREWORK DISPLAY. IN 2014, DUBAI BROKE THE GUINNESS WORLD RECORD FOR THE LARGEST FIREWORK DISPLAY, FIRING 479,651 SHELLS IN SIX MINUTES!

THE PALM JUMEIRAH IS DESIGNED TO LOOK LIKE A PALM TREE.

There are houses, hotels, shopping centers, and vacation homes on The Palm. Many people travel from all over the world to stay at this amazing place.

DESERTS

As well as amazing buildings, the Middle East also has some crazy natural landscapes, too. The Middle East is home to the second-largest hot desert in the world: the Arabian Desert! The Arabian Desert covers 888,035 miles (2,300,000 sq km) and spans Jordan, Iraq, Kuwait, Saudi Arabia, United Arab Emirates, Oman, and Yemen. The Arabian Desert contains one of the world's largest areas of sand. This is called the Rub'al-Khali.

Although it can get as hot as 131°F (55°C) in the Arabian Desert, some animals and insects still manage to live there. Locusts, dung beetles, scorpions, and spiders all live in this hot and sandy habitat. Other wildlife includes lizards and snakes. Sometimes even a gazelle can be spotted too!

DESERTS ARE NOT JUST HOT – SOME DESERTS ARE COLD! ANTARCTICA AND THE ARCTIC ARE THE LARGEST DESERTS IN THE WORLD!

THIS IS A DUNG BEETLE ROLLING A BALL OF ANIMAL POOP. YUCK!

A SAND GAZELLE

GLOSSARY

aromatic   something that smells sweet, or like perfume

Berber   a language spoken by the Berber people from northwestern Africa

cartographers   people who make maps

chemists   people who study chemicals and carry out experiments

civilizations   the societies, cultures, and ways of life of certain areas

coordinates   numbers that indicate a position on a line, usually on a map

cuneiform   a writing system used in Mesopotamia and Persia that is made up of wedge-shaped characters

cypress extracts   samples taken from the cypress tree

eclipses   when a planet, star, or moon is hidden by another, or by a shadow

ethnicities   groups of people that share a national or cultural tradition

extracting   removing or taking out

factors   numbers that we multiply together to make another number

hemispheres   sections of the Earth, either Northern, Southern, Eastern, or Western

iconic   well known and recognized around the world as a symbol of a place, time, or set of opinions

latitude   the distance north or south of the Equator, measured in degrees

lunar calendar   a calendar based on the orbit of the Moon

Mecca   the birthplace of Muhammad and the holiest city in Islam. Mecca is in Saudi Arabia

mental illness   medical disorders that affect a person's personality, mind, or emotions

orbit   the path that an object makes around a larger object in space

philosophy   the study of the nature of knowledge, reality, and existence

Pillar of Islam   a base of the Islamic faith, of which there are five

Ramadan   the month-long Islamic festival when Muslims do not eat during daylight hours

refracted   what happens to a ray of light when it passes through something that changes its speed

scented   made to smell nicely

secular   not related to anything religious or spiritual

settlements   places people live permanently and form communities, like villages or towns

sexagesimal   based on the number 60

surgical   using instruments and equipment to carry out operations on the body

symptoms   things that happen in the body suggesting that there is a disease or disorder

INDEX

Page 13 Answers: 1. 16, 2. 9,
3. 20, 4. 30, 5. 40